# America Says Goodbye to France:

## Pontiac's Rebellion, Proclamation of 1763

**U.S. Revolutionary Period Grade 4 |
Children's Military Books**

**BABY PROFESSOR**
EDUCATION KIDS

First Edition, 2020

Published in the United States by Speedy Publishing LLC, 40 E Main Street, Newark, Delaware 19711 USA.

Baby Professor Books are available at special discounts when purchased in bulk for industrial and sales-promotional use. For details contact our Special Sales Team at Speedy Publishing LLC, 40 E Main Street, Newark, Delaware 19711 USA. Telephone (888) 248-4521 Fax: (210) 519-4043.

10 9 8 7 6 * 5 4 3 2 1

Print Edition: 9781541959743
Digital Edition: 9781541962743
Hardcover Edition: 9781541979734

*See the world in pictures. Build your knowledge in style.*
*www.speedypublishing.com*

# Table Of Contents

Who was Pontiac and Why Did he Start a Rebellion? . . . . .15

Pontiac Forms a Confederacy. . . . . . . . . . . . . . . . . . . . . . . . . .27

The British Government's Response to the Rebellion . . . .39

The Effects of the Rebellion. . . . . . . . . . . . . . . . . . . . . . . . .55

Why do you think America would be saying goodbye to France? At one time in history, some European countries came to the North American continent. Two of these countries were Britain and France. The British came in pursuit of land, settling it and making a profit from it.

THE BRITISH CAME TO NORTH AMERICA
IN PURSUIT OF LAND.

FORT NIAGARA IS A FORTIFICATION ORIGINALLY BUILT TO PROTECT THE INTERESTS OF NEW FRANCE IN NORTH AMERICA.

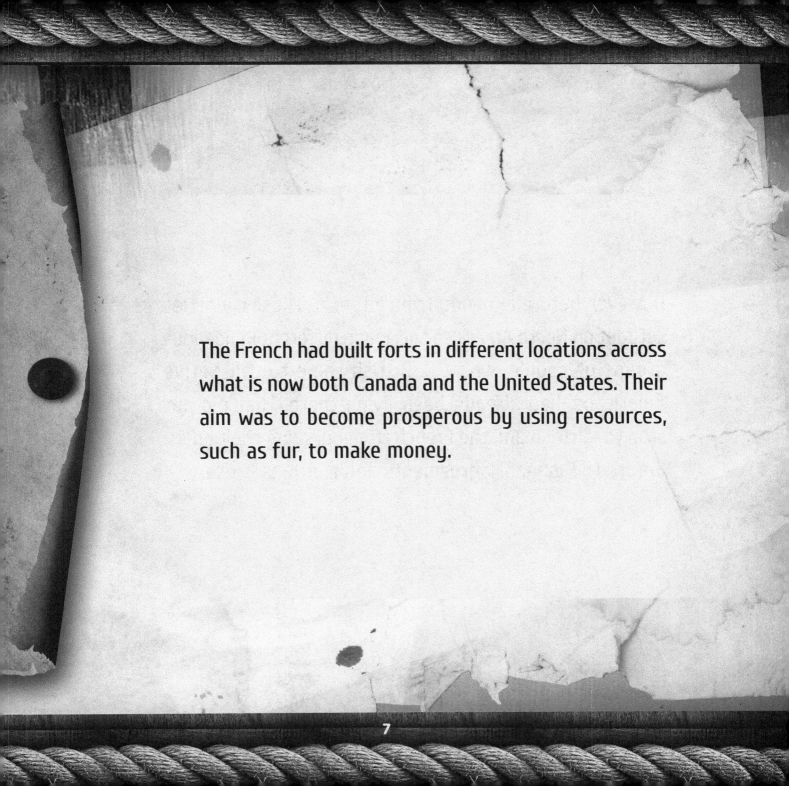

The French had built forts in different locations across what is now both Canada and the United States. Their aim was to become prosperous by using resources, such as fur, to make money.

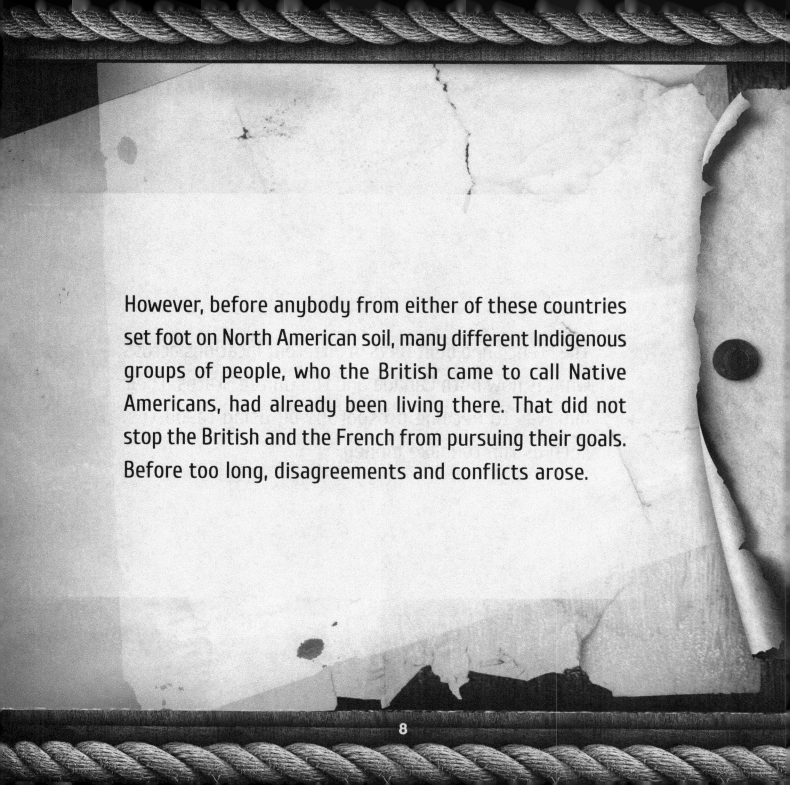

However, before anybody from either of these countries set foot on North American soil, many different Indigenous groups of people, who the British came to call Native Americans, had already been living there. That did not stop the British and the French from pursuing their goals. Before too long, disagreements and conflicts arose.

NATIVE AMERICANS

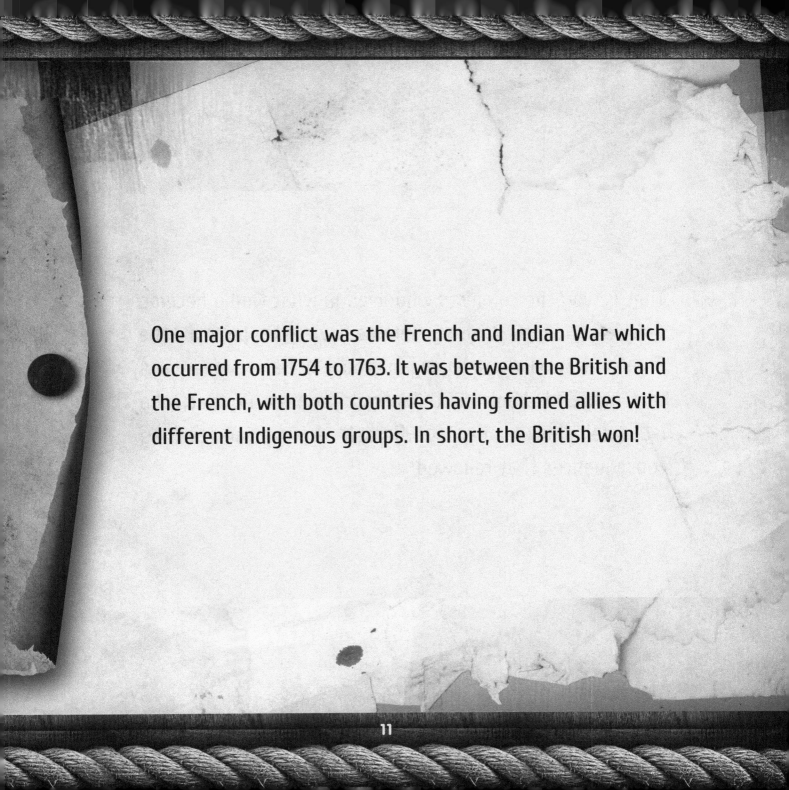

One major conflict was the French and Indian War which occurred from 1754 to 1763. It was between the British and the French, with both countries having formed allies with different Indigenous groups. In short, the British won!

That is why the colonists who lived in what would become America, and their British government, were happy to bid the French farewell. However, many groups of Native Americans remained. This book will talk about one man, Pontiac, who led a rebellion against the British and the far-reaching consequences that followed.

THE COLONISTS WERE HAPPY TO BID THE FRENCH FAREWELL.

# Who was Pontiac and Why Did he Start a Rebellion?

P ontiac was a Native American who was born in what is now Ohio sometime around 1720. He grew up to become a Chief of a Native American group known as the Ottawa people. They inhabited areas of land in the region of the Great Lakes.

PONTIAC

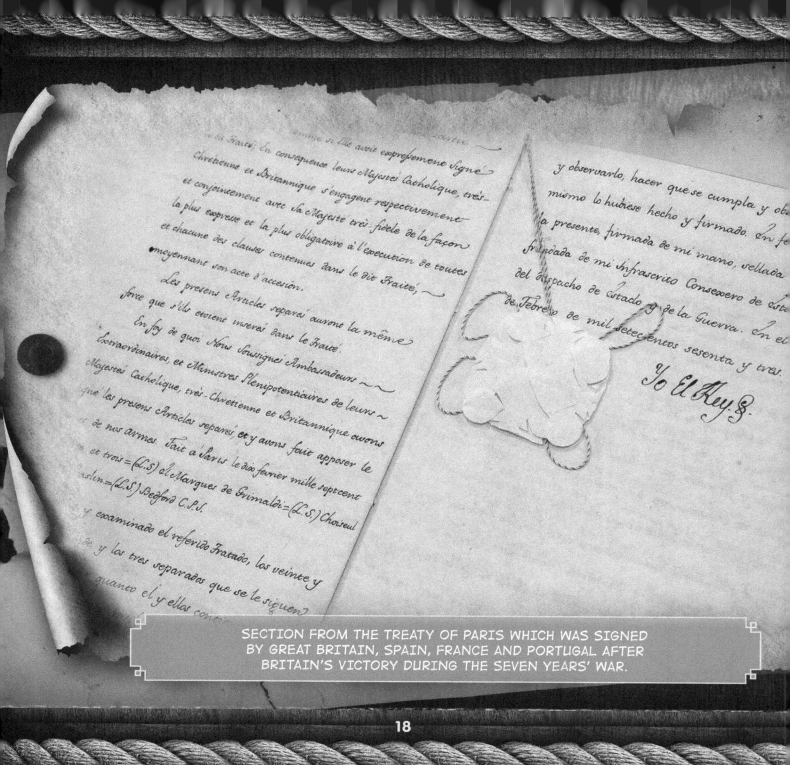

SECTION FROM THE TREATY OF PARIS WHICH WAS SIGNED
BY GREAT BRITAIN, SPAIN, FRANCE AND PORTUGAL AFTER
BRITAIN'S VICTORY DURING THE SEVEN YEARS' WAR.

After the end of the French and Indian War, the French and the British signed the Treaty of Paris, (not to be confused with the Treaty of Paris that would happen in 1783). This treaty signified that the war had officially come to an end and that Britain, as the victor, would gain control over New France. As the French had claimed parts of North America and given them the name, New France, signing this treaty now meant that the French would be leaving.

The departure of the French greatly concerned the Amerindians, a group of Native Americans. The French had made alliances with different tribes. Together they learned to live peacefully by trading with each other. Now that the French were leaving, the tribes would have to try to get along with the British who treated them quite differently.

FRENCH FUR TRADERS AND NATIVE AMERICANS DANCING
AT A RENDEZVOUS IN THE NORTH WOODS.

THE BRITISH DID NOT CONSIDER THE NATIVE
AMERICANS TO BE EQUAL PARTNERS IN THEIR LAND.

The British viewed North America as their land. They did not consider the Native Americans to be equal partners in this land. Now that the British had fought and won a costly war against the French for the land, they felt that they had full and exclusive rights to it. They started to make changes that the Amerindians considered to be both unreasonable and unfair.

Different laws and restrictions were enforced on the Amerindians. The Amerindians were not allowed to own their own firearms.

THE AMERINDIANS WERE NOT ALLOWED TO OWN THEIR OWN FIREARMS.

In addition to these laws, British colonists were starting to come in large numbers to settle. The Amerindians felt quite threatened. In addition to their rights, the land on which they had lived for thousands of years was being settled by the British.

BRITISH COLONISTS WERE STARTING TO COME IN LARGE NUMBERS TO SETTLE.

# Pontiac Forms a Confederacy

Pontiac did not like the fact that the British were making claims to the land that he did not feel rightfully belonged to them. He did his best to live peacefully with the British colonists but it soon became obvious that the British wanted complete control over all the land.

PONTIAC DID HIS BEST TO LIVE PEACEFULLY
WITH THE BRITISH COLONISTS.

To prevent the British from continuing to take even more land, he decided that the Native American tribes should come together and stand up to the colonial power.

PONTIAC DECIDED THAT THE NATIVE AMERICAN TRIBES SHOULD COME TOGETHER AND STAND UP TO THE COLONIAL POWER.

After all, the different Indigenous groups had been living on the land long before any Europeans came. Pontiac felt that it was time to force them to leave. The Ohio River Valley was rightfully the land of the Native Americans.

THE OHIO RIVER VALLEY WAS RIGHTFULLY
THE LAND OF THE NATIVE AMERICANS.

CHIEF PONTIAC ADDRESSING A GATHERING OF NATIVE
AMERICANS TO RALLY THEM AGAINST THE BRITISH.

Pontiac was able to persuade some of the tribes to join him in a confederacy. Together the confederacy was made up of different groups that formed the Iroquois, people from Delaware and members of the Shawnee who would join forces against the British. They felt that together, they had a good chance at fighting the British.

Pontiac and members of his confederacy started to fight back in 1763. By organizing different types of attacks and engaging in many battles, they were able to do a lot of damage to the British.

NATIVE AMERICANS ATTACKING AN OUTLYING PLANTATION IN COLONIAL MARYLAND.

They started fires on areas of the frontier on which the British had established settlements and they killed many of the British colonists.

NATIVE AMERICANS ATTACKING A CUMBERLAND VALLEY SETTLEMENT.

They also attacked and gained control over different British forts. When some other Native Americans who had not participated in the attacks learned of Pontiac's success, they too joined to fight the British. Sometimes, Pontiac would win battles against the British and sometimes, he would not.

CHIEF PONTIAC'S SIEGE OF FORT DETROIT.

# The British Government's Response to the Rebellion

The British government responded to Pontiac's Rebellion by sending in soldiers to fight. Henry Bouquet, a colonel in the British Army, was put in charge. They fought against Pontiac and his men. Although the British had suffered a lot of damage and loss, they managed to put a stop to the uprising.

HENRY BOUQUET

COLONEL HENRY BOUQUET IN COUNCIL WITH THE NATIVE AMERICAN
TRIBES ON THE BANKS OF THE MUSKINGUM RIVER IN OCTOBER 1764.

KING GEORGE III

However, Pontiac and the Confederacy were still seen as a threat. King George III, who ruled the American colonies from Britain, did not want to lose the financial benefits that the colonies brought to him.

There was a lot of money to be made from the fur trade, the furs of which were supplied from trade with the Native Americans, at the very place that Pontiac wanted! The king did not want anything to disrupt the fur trade. To keep the fur trade alive, the British would have to live peacefully with the Native Americans.

FUR TRADERS AND NATIVE AMERICANS

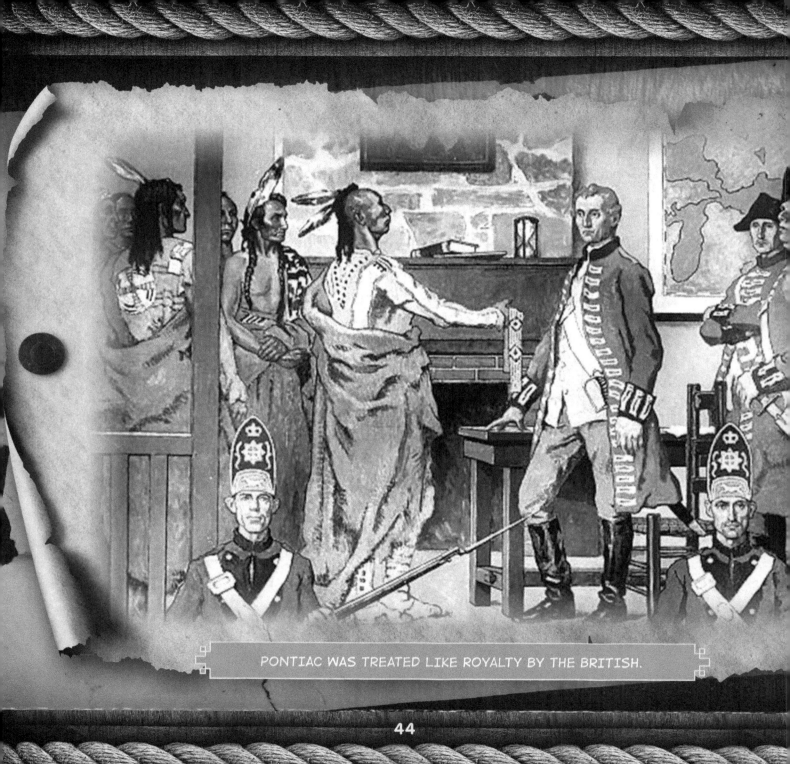

PONTIAC WAS TREATED LIKE ROYALTY BY THE BRITISH.

To appease Pontiac and his supporters, the king decided that something must be done. One obvious option would be to strengthen the British military force in the area. However, since Britain was in debt from the expenses that came from fighting in the French and Indian War, that was not what the king chose to do. Instead, he decided that he would win Pontiac's favor by being nice to him. Pontiac suddenly started to be treated like royalty by the British.

In addition to the doting and highly favored status bestowed on Pontiac, the king decided to enforce a royal proclamation that had already been decreed. While the proclamation was made following the French and Indian War, it really had not been carried out in principle. Now, it would be!

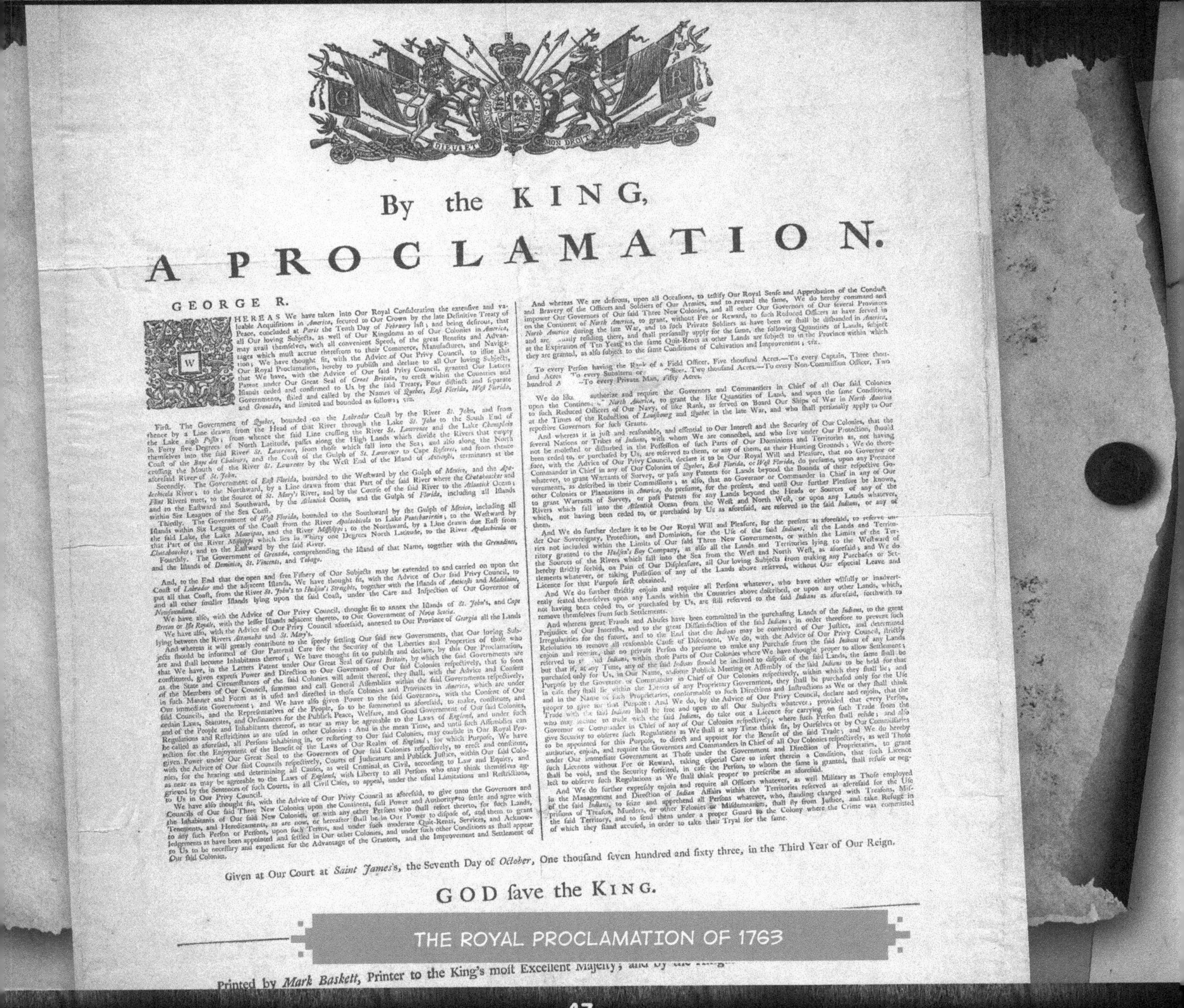

By the KING,

# A PROCLAMATION.

GEORGE R.

WHEREAS We have taken into Our Royal Consideration the extensive and valuable Acquisitions in *America*, secured to Our Crown by the late Definitive Treaty of Peace, concluded at *Paris* the Tenth Day of *February* last; and being desirous, that all Our loving Subjects, as well of Our Kingdoms as of Our Colonies in *America*, may avail themselves, with all convenient Speed, of the great Benefits and Advantages which must accrue therefrom to their Commerce, Manufactures, and Navigation; We have thought fit, with the Advice of Our Privy Council, to issue this Our Royal Proclamation, hereby to publish and declare to all Our loving Subjects, that We have, with the Advice of Our said Privy Council, granted Our Letters Patent under Our Great Seal of *Great Britain*, to erect within the Countries and Islands ceded and confirmed to Us by the said Treaty, Four distinct and separate Governments, stiled and called by the Names of *Quebec*, *East Florida*, *West Florida*, and *Grenada*, and limited and bounded as follows; viz.

First. The Government of *Quebec*, bounded on the *Labrador* Coast by the River *St. John*, and from thence by a Line drawn from the Head of that River through the Lake *St. John* to the South End of the Lake nigh *Pissin*; from whence the said Line crossing the River *St. Lawrence* and the Lake *Champlain* in Forty five Degrees of North Latitude, passes along the High Lands which divide the Rivers that empty themselves into the said River *St. Lawrence*, from those which fall into the Sea; and also along the North Coast of the *Baye des Chaleurs*, and the Coast of the Gulph of *St. Lawrence* to Cape *Rosieres*, and from thence crossing the Mouth of the River *St. Lawrence* by the West End of the Island of *Anticosti*, terminates at the aforesaid River of *St. John*.

Secondly. The Government of *East Florida*, bounded to the Westward by the Gulph of *Mexico*, and the *Apalachicola* River; to the Northward, by a Line drawn from that Part of the said River where the *Chatahouchee* and *Flint* Rivers meet, to the Source of *St. Mary's* River, and by the Course of the said River to the *Atlantick* Ocean; and to the Eastward and Southward, by the *Atlantick* Ocean, and the Gulph of *Florida*, including all Islands within Six Leagues of the Sea Coast.

Thirdly. The Government of *West Florida*, bounded to the Southward by the Gulph of *Mexico*, including all Islands within Six Leagues of the Coast from the River *Apalachicola* to Lake *Pontchartrain*; to the Westward by the said Lake, the Lake *Maurepas*, and the River *Mississippi*; to the Northward, by a Line drawn due East from that Part of the River *Mississippi* which lies in Thirty one Degrees North Latitude, to the River *Apalachicola* or *Chatahouchee*; and to the Eastward by the said River.

Fourthly. The Government of *Grenada*, comprehending the Island of that Name, together with the *Grenadines*, and the Islands of *Dominico*, *St. Vincents*, and *Tobago*.

And, to the End that the open and free Fishery of Our Subjects may be extended to and carried on upon the Coast of *Labrador* and the adjacent Islands, We have thought fit, with the Advice of Our said Privy Council, to put all that Coast, from the River *St. John's* to *Hudson's Streights*, together with the Islands of *Anticosti* and *Madelaine*, and all other smaller Islands lying upon the said Coast, under the Care and Inspection of Our Governor of *Newfoundland*.

We have also, with the Advice of Our Privy Council, thought fit to annex the Islands of *St. John's*, and *Cape Breton* or *Isle Royale*, with the lesser Islands adjacent thereto, to Our Government of *Nova Scotia*.

We have also, with the Advice of Our Privy Council aforesaid, annexed to Our Province of *Georgia* all the Lands lying between the Rivers *Altamaha* and *St. Mary's*.

And whereas it will greatly contribute to the speedy settling Our said new Governments, that Our loving Subjects should be informed of Our Paternal Care for the Security of the Liberties and Properties of those who are and shall become Inhabitants thereof; We have thought fit to publish and declare, by this Our Proclamation, that We have, in the Letters Patent under Our Great Seal of *Great Britain*, by which the said Governments are constituted, given express Power and Direction to Our Governors of Our said Colonies respectively, that so soon as the State and Circumstances of the said Colonies will admit thereof, they shall, with the Advice and Consent of the Members of Our Council, summon and call General Assemblies within the said Governments respectively, in such Manner and Form as is used and directed in those Colonies and Provinces in *America*, which are under Our immediate Government; and We have also given Power to the said Governors, with the Consent of Our said Councils, and the Representatives of the People, so to be summoned as aforesaid, to make, constitute, and ordain Laws, Statutes, and Ordinances for the Publick Peace, Welfare, and Good Government of Our said Colonies, and of the People and Inhabitants thereof, as near as may be agreeable to the Laws of *England*, and under such Regulations and Restrictions as are used in other Colonies: And in the mean Time, and until such Assemblies can be called as aforesaid, all Persons inhabiting in, or resorting to Our said Colonies, may confide in Our Royal Protection for the Enjoyment of the Benefit of the Laws of Our Realm of *England*; for which Purpose, We have given Power under Our Great Seal to the Governors of Our said Colonies respectively, to erect and constitute, with the Advice of Our said Councils respectively, Courts of Judicature and Publick Justice, within Our said Colonies, for the hearing and determining all Causes, as well Criminal as Civil, according to Law and Equity, and as near as may be agreeable to the Laws of *England*, with Liberty to all Persons who may think themselves aggrieved by the Sentences of such Courts, in all Civil Cases, to appeal, under the usual Limitations and Restrictions, to Us in Our Privy Council.

We have also thought fit, with the Advice of Our Privy Council as aforesaid, to give unto the Governors and Councils of Our said Three New Colonies upon the Continent, full Power and Authority to settle and agree with the Inhabitants of Our said New Colonies, or with any other Persons who shall resort thereto, for such Lands, Tenements, and Hereditaments, as are now, or hereafter shall be in Our Power to dispose of, and them to grant to any such Person or Persons, upon such Terms, and under such moderate Quit-Rents, Services, and Acknowledgements as have been appointed and settled in Our other Colonies, and under such other Conditions as shall appear to Us to be necessary and expedient for the Advantage of the Grantees, and the Improvement and Settlement of Our said Colonies.

And whereas We are desirous, upon all Occasions, to testify Our Royal Sense and Approbation of the Conduct and Bravery of the Officers and Soldiers of Our Armies, and to reward the same, We do hereby command and impower Our Governors of Our said Three New Colonies, and all other Our Governors of Our several Provinces on the Continent of *North America*, to grant, without Fee or Reward, to such Reduced Officers as have served in *North America* during the late War, and to such Private Soldiers as have been or shall be disbanded in *America*, and are actually residing there, and shall personally apply for the same, the following Quantities of Lands, subject at the Expiration of Ten Years to the same Quit-Rents as other Lands are subject to in the Province within which they are granted, as also subject to the same Conditions of Cultivation and Improvement; viz.

To every Person having the Rank of a Field Officer, Five thousand Acres.—To every Captain, Three thousand Acres.—To every Subaltern or Staff Officer, Two thousand Acres.—To every Non-Commission Officer, Two hundred Acres.—To every Private Man, Fifty Acres.

We do likewise authorize and require the Governors and Commanders in Chief of all Our said Colonies upon the Continent of *North America*, to grant the like Quantities of Land, and upon the same Conditions, to such Reduced Officers of Our Navy, of like Rank, as served on Board Our Ships of War in *North America* at the Times of the Reduction of *Louisbourg* and *Quebec* in the late War, and who shall personally apply to Our respective Governors for such Grants.

And whereas it is just and reasonable, and essential to Our Interest and the Security of Our Colonies, that the several Nations or Tribes of *Indians*, with whom We are connected, and who live under Our Protection, should not be molested or disturbed in the Possession of such Parts of Our Dominions and Territories as, not having been ceded to, or purchased by Us, are reserved to them, or any of them, as their Hunting Grounds; We do therefore, with the Advice of Our Privy Council, declare it to be Our Royal Will and Pleasure, that no Governor or Commander in Chief in any of Our Colonies of *Quebec*, *East Florida*, or *West Florida*, do presume, upon any Pretence whatever, to grant Warrants of Survey, or pass any Patents for Lands beyond the Bounds of their respective Governments, as described in their Commissions; as also, that no Governor or Commander in Chief in any of Our other Colonies or Plantations in *America*, do presume, for the present, and until Our further Pleasure be known, to grant Warrants of Survey, or pass Patents for any Lands beyond the Heads or Sources of any of the Rivers which fall into the *Atlantick* Ocean from the West and North West, or upon any Lands whatever, which, not having been ceded to, or purchased by Us as aforesaid, are reserved to the said *Indians*, or any of them.

And We do further declare it to be Our Royal Will and Pleasure, for the present as aforesaid, to reserve under Our Sovereignty, Protection, and Dominion, for the Use of the said *Indians*, all the Lands and Territories not included within the Limits of Our said Three New Governments, or within the Limits of the Territory granted to the *Hudson's Bay* Company, as also all the Lands and Territories lying to the Westward of the Sources of the Rivers which fall into the Sea from the West and North West, as aforesaid; and We do hereby strictly forbid, on Pain of Our Displeasure, all Our loving Subjects from making any Purchases or Settlements whatever, or taking Possession of any of the Lands above reserved, without Our especial Leave and Licence for that Purpose first obtained.

And We do further strictly enjoin and require all Persons whatever, who have either wilfully or inadvertently seated themselves upon any Lands within the Countries above described, or upon any other Lands, which, not having been ceded to, or purchased by Us, are still reserved to the said *Indians* as aforesaid, forthwith to remove themselves from such Settlements.

And whereas great Frauds and Abuses have been committed in the purchasing Lands of the *Indians*, to the great Prejudice of Our Interests, and to the great Dissatisfaction of the said *Indians*; in order therefore to prevent such Irregularities for the future, and to the End that the *Indians* may be convinced of Our Justice, and determined Resolution to remove all reasonable Cause of Discontent, We do, with the Advice of Our Privy Council, strictly enjoin and require, that no private Person do presume to make any Purchase from the said *Indians* of any Lands reserved to the said *Indians*, within those Parts of Our Colonies where We have thought proper to allow Settlement; but that if, at any Time, any of the said *Indians* should be inclined to dispose of the said Lands, the same shall be purchased only for Us, in Our Name, at some Publick Meeting or Assembly of the said *Indians* to be held for that Purpose by the Governor or Commander in Chief of Our Colonies respectively, within which they shall lie; and in case they shall lie within the Limits of any Proprietary Government, they shall be purchased only for the Use and in the Name of such Proprietaries, conformable to such Directions and Instructions as We or they shall think proper to give for that Purpose: And We do, by the Advice of Our Privy Council, declare and enjoin, that the Trade with the said *Indians* shall be free and open to all Our Subjects whatever; provided that every Person, who may incline to trade with the said *Indians*, do take out a Licence for carrying on such Trade from the Governor or Commander in Chief of any of Our Colonies respectively, where such Person shall reside; and also give Security to observe such Regulations as We shall at any Time think fit, by Ourselves or by Our Commissaries to be appointed for this Purpose, to direct and appoint for the Benefit of the said Trade; and We do hereby authorize, enjoin, and require the Governors and Commanders in Chief of all Our Colonies respectively, as well Those under Our immediate Government as Those under the Government and Direction of Proprietaries, to grant such Licences without Fee or Reward, taking especial Care to insert therein a Condition, that such Licence shall be void, and the Security forfeited, in case the Person, to whom the same is granted, shall refuse or neglect to observe such Regulations as We shall think proper to prescribe as aforesaid.

And We do further expressly enjoin and require all Officers whatever, as well Military as Those employed in the Management and Direction of *Indian* Affairs within the Territories reserved as aforesaid for the Use of the said *Indians*, to seize and apprehend all Persons whatever, who, standing charged with Treasons, Misprisions of Treason, Murders, or other Felonies or Misdemeanors, shall fly from Justice, and take Refuge in the said Territory, and to send them under a proper Guard to the Colony where the Crime was committed of which they stand accused, in order to take their Tryal for the same.

Given at Our Court at *Saint James's*, the Seventh Day of *October*, One thousand seven hundred and sixty three, in the Third Year of Our Reign.

GOD save the KING.

Printed by *Mark Baskett*, Printer to the King's most Excellent Majesty; and by the ...

THE ROYAL PROCLAMATION OF 1763

HUDSON   BAY COMPANY                    49°                              N S

                                                              (to Mass)

                                                                    N H

PROVINCE OF                                              N Y    MASS
QUEBEC
                                                                       R I
                                  Proclamation Line of 1763   PA      N J    CONN

                                                            MD      DEL
(Spain)
                                                     VA

INDIAN                                                    N C
RESERVE
                                                    S C

                                              GA

W FLA

                                                    E FLA

THE DEFINED BOUNDARIES BETWEEN THE BRITISH
THIRTEEN COLONIES AND THE BACKCOUNTRY
FOLLOWING THE PROCLAMATION OF 1763.

The proclamation would establish clear living boundaries for both the colonists and the Native Americans within the frontier. Land to the west of the Appalachian Mountains would be allotted to the Native American groups. The colonists who had already settled there were ordered to abandon the area. This decree was made in 1763 and it became known as the Royal Proclamation of 1763 or simply the Proclamation of 1763.

The king and his men who ruled from Britain thought that this proclamation was a great way to settle matters. They believed that it would show the Native Americans that the British were a decent group of people. This would be done through the British giving back land that had been taken from the Indigenous peoples. Once the land was back in the hands of the Native Americans, they would in turn, trade fur with the British.

NATIVE AMERICANS TRADING FUR WITH THE BRITISH.

VIEW OF THE APPALACHIAN MOUNTAINS NEAR THE STATE
BORDERS OF NORTH CAROLINA AND TENNESSEE

They also assumed that the colonists would have no trouble accepting the terms of settling east of the Appalachian Mountains because the land west of it, as far as the British government was concerned, was not suitable for farming. The British, who ruled a colony from across an ocean, were about to discover that their assumptions were incorrect!

# The Effects of
# the Rebellion

Neither the colonists nor the Native Americans were pleased with the terms of the Royal Proclamation that was suddenly being enforced. The colonists were deeply disappointed because they were the ones who helped fight for the land in the French and Indian War. After all the sacrifice and loyalty shown to the British monarchy, they were now being told that they could not settle in the area of their choice. To them, this was completely unacceptable.

THE COLONISTS WERE DEEPLY DISAPPOINTED
WITH THE TERMS OF THE ROYAL PROCLAMATION.

THE COLONISTS CONSIDERED THE LAND WEST OF THE
APPALACHIAN MOUNTAINS TO BE SUITABLE FOR FARMING.

Furthermore, while the king and the rest of the leaders in Britain may not have chosen the land west of the Appalachian Mountains, many colonists certainly did. The British leaders in Britain had no idea about the quality of the land because they were miles away. They thought that it was a bleak frontier with little to offer in the way of farming. The colonists, however, considered it to be very fertile and suitable for farming.

Moreover, many of them had already settled there. Having to give up their new life in the settlements was not something that they were prepared to do. A lot of people defied the king's orders in the proclamation and chose to live where they pleased. The colonists were starting to feel more and more distant from the British government who ruled from afar. To them, the king and his government cared very little about the people living in the colonies.

EVEN AFTER BRITAIN ISSUED THE ROYAL PROCLAMATION OF 1763, COLONISTS CONTINUED TO SETTLE IN THE AREAS WEST OF THE APPALACHIAN MOUNTAINS.

THE NATIVE AMERICANS FELT THAT THE BRITISH
WERE ONLY TRYING TO APPEASE PONTIAC.

As for the Native Americans, they were not pleased with the terms of the proclamation either. Many of them felt that the British were only trying to appease Pontiac without showing a genuine interest in the concerns of other Native American groups. Gradually, their dissatisfaction and anger with the British became directed at Pontiac. They resented that he was being treated so well while others, who had fought beside him, were being ignored.

Although Pontiac's Rebellion was an organized conflict that had resulted in some victories for his people, in 1766, tired of fighting, Pontiac entered a peace treaty with the British. They both hoped to put an end to the conflict and hard feelings. After all that had happened, this gesture was not enough to stop the anger and frustration of some of the Native Americans.

PONTIAC ENTERED A PEACE TREATY WITH THE BRITISH.

THE DEATH OF
PONTIAC IN 1769.

The resentment continued to grow as time went on and in 1769, Pontiac was assassinated by a Peoria fighter. The assassination resulted in a lot of upheaval and conflict among different Native Americans. The confederacy that Pontiac had formed came to an end. There was no unifying power to keep it in place. The different Native American tribes could not agree on how to move forward.

Even though the British had said goodbye to the French after winning the French and Indian War, they still had their share of problems. Relations with different Native American groups was far from perfect. Without close ties with the Native Americans, conducting the fur trade would be much more challenging.

As for the relationship between the British government and members of its colonies in North America, things were not as they should have been. Many colonists felt that their government in Britain was doing nothing to take care of their needs.

Although the British had said goodbye to the French, could it be possible that they would also have to say goodbye to their colonies in North America? Find out more about what happened in other Baby Professor books about the American Revolution.

# Visit

## www.speedypublishing.com

To view and download free content
on your favorite subject and browse
our catalog of new and exciting
books for readers of all ages.

CPSIA information can be obtained
at www.ICGtesting.com
Printed in the USA
BVHW062322301121
622797BV00005B/96